Christmas Around the World

Christmas in

Australia

By Christina Earley

Table of Contents

A Starfish Book

Teaching Tips for Caregivers:

As a caregiver, you can help your child succeed in school by giving them a strong foundation in language and literacy skills and a desire to learn to read.

This book helps children grow by letting them practice reading skills.

Reading for pleasure and interest will help your child to develop reading skills and will give your child the opportunity to practice these skills in meaningful ways.

- Encourage your child to read on her own at home
- Encourage your child to practice reading aloud
- Encourage activities that require reading
- Establish a reading time
- Talk with your child
- Give your child writing materials

Teaching Tips for Teachers:

Research shows that one of the best ways for students to learn a new topic is to read about it.

Before Reading

- Read the "Words to Know" and discuss the meaning of each word.
- Read the back cover to see what the book is about.

During Reading

- When a student gets to a word that is unknown, ask them to look at the rest of the sentence to find clues to help with the meaning of the unknown word.
- Ask the student to write down any pages of the book that were confusing to them.

After Reading

- Discuss the main idea of the book.
- Ask students to give one detail that they learned in the book by showing a text dependent answer from the book.

Christmas in

Australia

HAPPY CHRISTMAS

HAPPY CHRISTMAS

HAPPY CHRISTMAS

Many people in Australia celebrate Christmas.

December is summer in Australia.
Some families go to the beach.

Homes are decorated with trees and **wreaths**. People also use the Christmas bush.

Fun Fact:
The Christmas bush has flowers that turn red near Christmas.

Carols by Candlelight is a **fundraiser** for children with vision problems.

People hold candles while singing.

Famous people also sing.

Santa Claus wears swim shorts and flip-flops.

He uses the front **porch** to get inside.

Children leave cake or cookies for Santa on Christmas Eve.

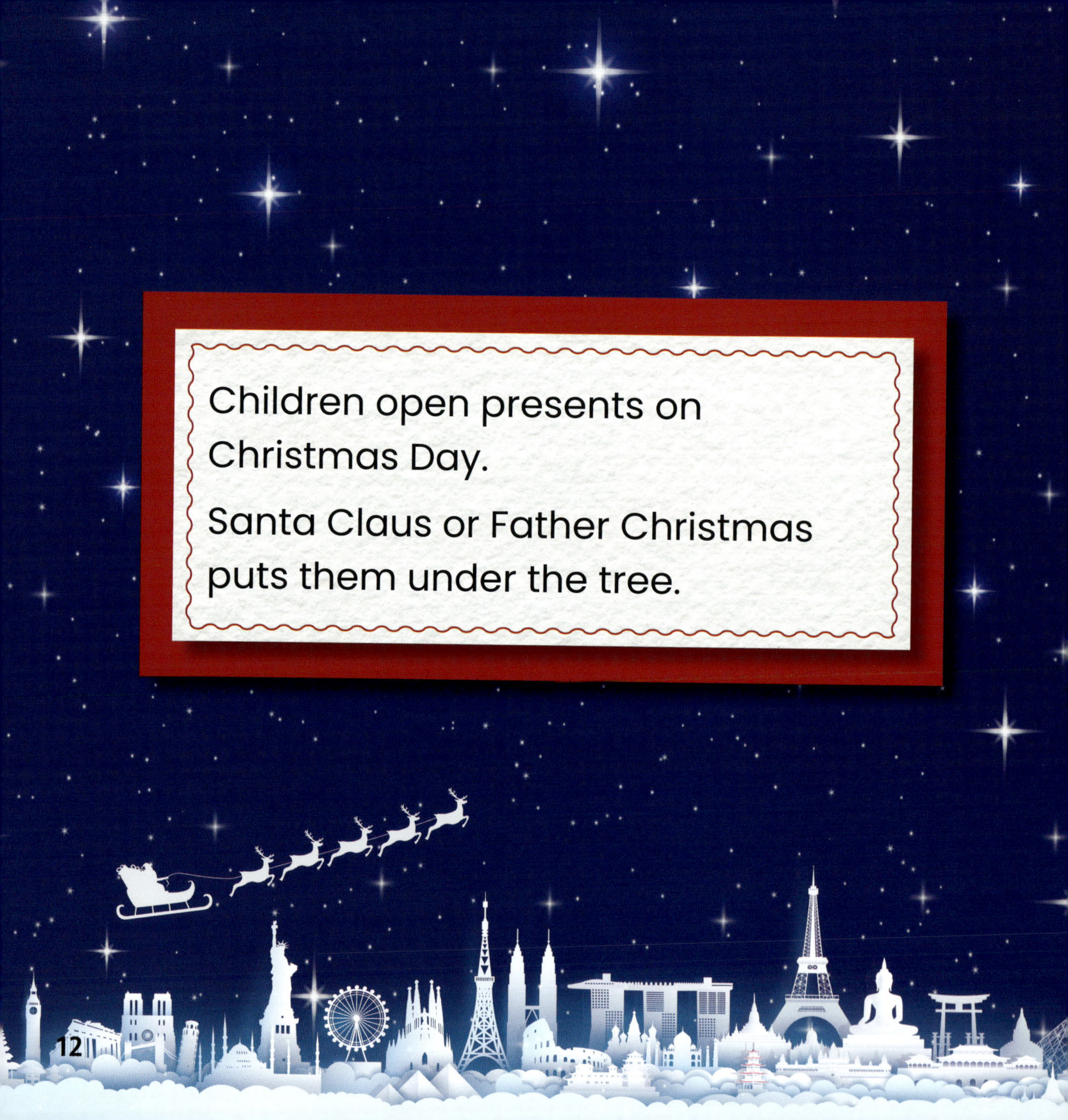

Children open presents on Christmas Day.

Santa Claus or Father Christmas puts them under the tree.

Families gather for lunch on Christmas day. They might eat **prawns**, a popular seafood. Pavlova is a cold dessert with fruit.

BOXING DAY
BOXING DAY
BOXING DAY

Boxing Day is December 26th.

Friends and families play **cricket**.

Some people celebrate Christmas again in July.

Then, it is winter and cold.

People can enjoy hot chocolate.

Fun Fact:
This celebration is called Yuletide or Yulefest.

Craft: Eucalyptus Christmas Wreath

Materials

- circular paper plate
- scissors
- 50 or more eucalyptus leaves (real or fake)
- glue
- small Christmas decorations or bow (optional)
- hole punch
- narrow ribbon

Steps

1. Cut a large hole in the center of the paper plate to create a wreath shape.
2. Glue individual eucalyptus leaves on the plate.
3. Add the decorations and bow.
4. Punch a hole in the top of the wreath. Thread the ribbon through the hole. Tie the ends together to make a loop for hanging.

Recipe: Pavlova

Ingredients

- 4 egg whites
- 1¼ cups superfine white sugar
- 1 teaspoon vanilla extract
- 1 teaspoon lemon juice
- 2 teaspoons cornstarch
- 1 pint heavy cream
- 2 cups cut-up fresh fruit such as kiwi, mango, strawberries, pineapple, and cherries

Steps

1. Preheat oven to 350° F (177° C). Line a baking sheet with parchment paper. Draw a 9-inch (23-centimeter) circle on the parchment paper.
2. In a large bowl, beat egg whites until stiff. Gradually add in the sugar and beat well after each addition.
3. Beat until thick and glossy.
4. Gently fold in the vanilla extract, lemon juice, and cornstarch.
5. Spoon mixture inside the circle on the parchment paper. Spread the mixture from the center toward the outside edge, building up the edge slightly. There should be a slight depression in the center.
6. Bake for 1 hour. Cool on a wire rack.
7. Beat the heavy cream in a small bowl until stiff peaks form.
8. Remove the meringue from the paper. Put on a flat serving plate.
9. Fill the center with the whipped cream. Top with fresh fruit.

Words to Know

Boxing Day (BAHKS-ing day): a holiday celebrated after Christmas Day, usually on December 26th

cricket (KRIK-it): a game played by two teams with smooth, flat bats and a small, hard ball

fundraiser (FUHND-ray-zur): an event to make money to give to a charity

porch (porch): a covered shelter in front of a house

prawns (prahnz): crustaceans that live in the sea and are similar to large shrimp

wreaths (reeths): groups of flowers, leaves, or branches twisted together in the shape of a circle

Index

Comprehension Questions

1. It is ____ in Australia during the Christmas season.
   a. winter
   b. spring
   c. summer

2. Santa's sleigh is sometimes pulled by
   a. koalas.
   b. elves.
   c. kangaroos.

3. Pavlova is a kind of
   a. dessert.
   b. seafood.
   c. drink.

4. True or false: Some celebrate Christmas again in July.

5. True or false: The Christmas bush has purple flowers.

Answers
1. c 2. c 3. a 4. True 5. False

About the Author

Christina Earley lives in South Florida with her with husband, son, and dog named Bailey. Her favorite holiday is Christmas because it is a magical time of year. She collects ornaments that remind her of special places and events. She and her family have lots of fun baking cookies and eating candy canes while looking at Christmas lights.

Written by: Christina Earley
Design by: Jen Bowers
Editor: Kim Thompson

Photographs: Cover © 2019 Kosit/Shutterstock, pine ©Pasko Maksim/Shutterstock,world skyline ©Painterstock/Shutterstock, background ©ghenadie/Shutterstock, earth ©leonello/iStock; p.1 ©Mariana Mast/Shutterstock; p.3 ©2020 LennartK95/Shutterstock; p.5 ©2018 Rawpixel.com/Shutterstock; p.7 ©2013 3523studio/ Shutterstock, ©2017 Michael Leslie/Shutterstock, ornament©ekler/ Shutterstock; p.9 ©2021 Marcos Castillo/Shutterstock; p.10 ©Christos Georghiou/Shutterstock; p.11 ©2017 Alfa Photostudio/ Shutterstock, ©2012 Julien Tromeur/Shutterstock; p.13 ©2018 Ekaterina Kupeeva/Shutterstock; p.14 ©2018 jr.photography16/ Shutterstock; p.16 ©2018 Tap10/Shutterstock, ©2014 Pepj/ Shutterstock; p.19 ©2015 Elena Shashkina/Shutterstock; p.20 ©2013 Mega Pixel/Shutterstock, ©2017 Robyn Mackenzie/ Shutterstock; p.21 ©2017 jackmazur/Shutterstock

Library of Congress PCN Data
Christmas in Australia / Earley
Christmas Around the World
ISBN 978-1-63897-446-8 (hard cover)
ISBN 978-1-63897-561-8 (paperback)
ISBN 978-1-63897-676-9 (EPUB)
ISBN 978-1-63897-791-9 (eBook)
Library of Congress Control Number: 2022930317

Printed in the United States of America.

Seahorse Publishing Company
www.seahorsepub.com

Published in the United States
Seahorse Publishing
PO Box 771325
Coral Springs, FL 33077